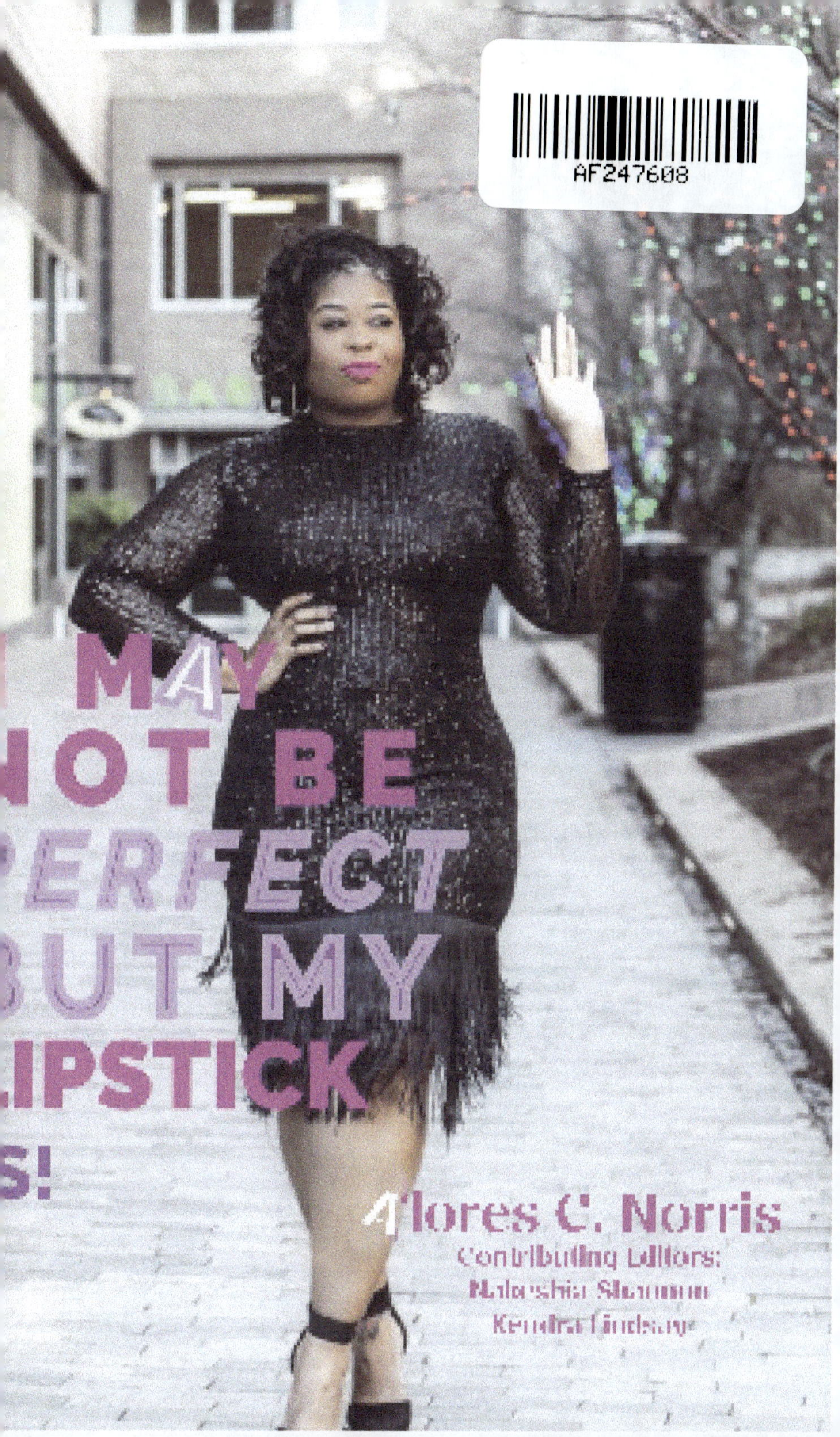

AF247608
I MAY
NOT BE
PERFECT
BUT MY
LIPSTICK
IS!
Flores C. Norris
Contributing Editors:
Nakeshia Shannon
Kendra Lindsay

Dedication

You were emotional but always my rock. I can tell when you were tired but you always kept going. You were worried but always full of hope. Impatient, yet patient. When you were overwhelmed you never quit. You were wonderful even in the middle of all this chaos.. You were my life changer every single day... I love you always mom.

Xoxo

Dir. Of Marketing
Turned MUA

Featured in Black Enterprise, Entrepreneur, The Root as the Top 50 Influencers.

www. MakeUpMogulUniversity.com
IG: @TiyanaRobinsonBeauty

As a mentor to A'Lores, I can say that her journey to success can be described as nothing short of INCREDIBLE, and she shares it in this book in a way that's transparent honest and RELATABLE. This book is a must-read if you're starting a business and want REAL TALK about what it takes to make it to the top.

The good, the bad, the ugly *AND* the pretty.

This Book is a must read if you're starting a business.

**CEO of Maven Media Management
My Life...Your Entertainment**

**www.MavenMediaManagement.com
IG: Danni_The_Maven**

A'Lores is truly a self-made moral; the world needs to be inspired by her story, her testimony, and her journey. I've had the pleasure of watching A'Lores grow her beauty brand from the ground up... Since day one. Like fine wine she just keeps getting better with time. Every black woman on a mission to make their dreams a reality needs to read this book.

Readers will be motivated and entertained! But, most importantly they will have a practical guide on how to create a legacy and become a brand.

A'Lores is truly a self made mogul; the world needs to be inspired by her story.

Public Relations & Personal Branding.
Formal Television Anchor and News Reporter

www.CrawfordStrategy.com

I met A'Lores by total chance on a day that I really needed a pick me up. Insert a mall makeup counter, this FABULOUS makeup artist who would become a dear friend, and the best makeover of my life. I knew on that day that this woman - this talented, driven artist - was destined for greatness.
Over the course of the next five years, she was more than just my MUA of choice getting me ready for national tv appearances, galas, and speaking events.
I was thrilled to watch her ascent to a successful businesswoman and entrepreneur. Now, she is turning her experiences into a riveting read that is equal parts Tell-All and How-To. Like a good lipstick shade can make an entire outfit.

Alores's book is a must have on any entrepreneurs bookshelf.

Just a badass Woman with more FAITH than fear!!!

Three years ago I began to think about owning my own boutique, but I was extremely unqualified, didn't know the first thing about management, or owning a business. I was a stay at home mom for 9 years so my work experience was little to none. While living in Germany in 2004, I started studying traditional makeup applications and eventually got my certification. After we left Germany my family and I moved to Oklahoma and I picked up a little clientele here and there, but my makeup skills were not where I wanted them to be, and Youtube was NOT educating me on the artistry nor the business side of what I really wanted to do with this makeup thing. That's what I called it at the time.

I made the decision to go back to college. While my husband was deployed and my three boys were in school I attended Cameron University majoring in StudioArts. This is where my makeup turned into art and my art turned into my vision. This is where I started to see and understand the true meaning of color theory, hue difference, warm vs. cool, the behaviors of color mixtures.

Majoring in studio arts is where I fell in love with Renaissance Art, gazed into the eyes of Rococo Art for hours from my art books and daydreamed about me being Leonid Afremov, but I was not that talent in painting. LOL! I was okay, but no where near that good.

I would never be Leonid Afremov. I could never pick up a few painters' knives and some oil paint on a blank canvas and turn it into a powerful breathtaking masterpiece, but I could study every style of painting, work on what I could do and apply it to my form of art and turn it into my own masterpiece.

Years later I toyed with the idea of me having my own. Never really believing that I could do it. I kinda pushed it in the back of my mind. Applied for makeup counter after makeup counter until finally being hired at one. Quickly realizing that artistry wasn't the main goal of the counter and continuing to be over-looked for full time positions that I deserved and being told, "Well A'Lores... You are just the talent and I'm not sure full time would be good for your right now."

So I **QUIT.** 2 weeks notice. Kiss my talented behind... **I'M OUT!**

After that I did a little freelance here and there. I also worked for another makeup counter, but I always knew that there was something more I wanted. ***My Own Studio*** Something small and cute. A couple of chairs and mirrors. Nothing big, and that's what I did. I quit the makeup counter job I had and went out on my own. Clients are booming. My nose in the air. Money coming in ! Working on my lipstick line! HAAA! Nobody can tell me nothing! Then **BOOM! I FAILED... just. like. that.**

Shut down. Door closed. Moved Out. Gone. How in God's name did that just happen? I had fallen and literally did not think I was going to get back up. Once again the thought of me hav-ing my own crossed my mind. But I couldn't do that! I just failed at it the first time and the funds were NOT there. I have a family. I simply can not continue to quit jobs and put all of this burden on my husband. So, I had a **LONG** talk with God.

I knew it was time for me to talk to him. I had been ignoring him
for a while. I thought I could do it all on my own. I went in my
closet and prayed, cried, screamed, kicked and hollered WHY?!
Why would you close that door on me? I was having os much of
a temper tantrum I couldn't see that he was trying to prepare
me for my own but BIGGER. After my temper tantrum with God I
began to shut up and listen. Move when He told me to and be
still when He said it.

I started meditating and working on the life I wanted
for myself and for my family. I started to work on my relationship with God. The more and more I worked on my
relationship with Him the more he showed me the door he
closed was for my protection. That was never my door to
begin with.

Nine months later I signed the lease to my cosmetic store
with God on one side and my husband on the other. This is
only the **BEGINNING** of my story.

**Meet the Owner and Creator of The House of Flawless
Makeup and Beauty Lounge.
A' Lores C. Norris.**

 **@FLAWLESSBEAUTYMAKEUP1**    **@ALORESHOUSEOFFLAWLESS**

WWW.THEHOUSEOFFLAWLESS.COM

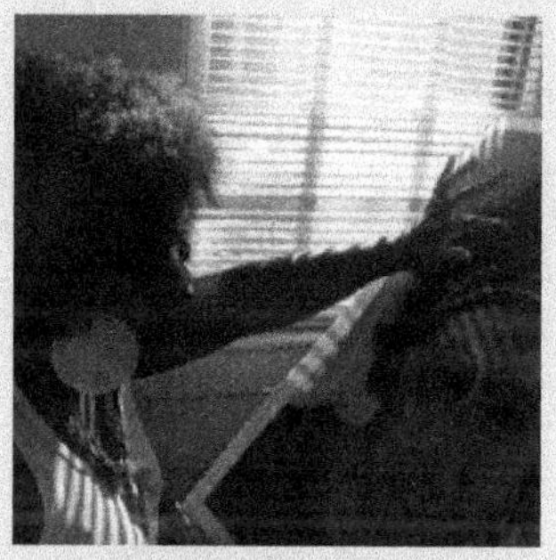

Content Pages

Content Pages

Chapter 1
ON A BAD DAY THERE IS ALWAYS LIPSTICK
We are Quarantined Gurl!

If any of you who are reading this book had a conversation with me you know that I have a down south Geehee Accent and it comes out when I'm stressed, mad or excited. What I want you to do is read this chapter in a South Carolina, Geechee Girl accent.

Listen to me Churin! We are in a crisis! Around the world people are sick, kids are out of school, businesses are closed, Walmart, Target, Sams, Publix and Bi-Lo are out of toilet paper type crisis!!!! WHAAA! (Not what...Remember you're reading this in my Geechee dialect) When I tell you I didn't see this coming! This thing literally knocked me off my feet. Mentally, and physically.

The House of Flawless just got herself back together. She survived the winter drought, along with a new makeup over the month of January. February we celebrated our 3rd year anniversary and the party was amazing! It snowed that night and people still showed up and showed out!

The beginning of March appointments were booming, bridal trials were booked and wedding dates were locked in. Prom girls had their prom dates together and our calendar was fully booked. Let's not forget the store was selling out of lipsticks, foundations and our new makeup brushes!

The House of Flawless girls and I did a new commercial and we were all cute and snatched!!! Honey, we had it going on! Then boom! CORONA VIRUS (read that part in CardiB's voice) Chileee, Corona came in here and tore The House of Flawless UP! Brides dropped, proms were cancelled and schools closed for the rest of the academic year. Customers stopped coming in. It went from 100 to 0 REAL quick and I panicked. I ran around the damn shop like I was crazy! I yelled and screamed! I cried I threw myself on the shop floor and rolled around for a minute!! Babbbbbaeeeee!!! I didn't know what to do. I allowed customers and clients to call and vent about their events being cancelled. I wasn't upset at all but I was worried. How in the heck am I going to get through this? Could The House of Flawless stand this type of hit? Hell, by the time this book comes out we may still be quarantined in the house so I guess we will see. LOL!!

Pause... Are you guys still reading this in my geechie Kingstree accent??? Yes??? GOOD!

After getting myself together from that four year old meltdown I said, "Okay, What will I do next? Damage control? I started reaching out via email to people with appointments letting them know we have officially been shut down and letting them know that they can always reschedule their appointments and/or get some amazing House of Flawless products sent to you. When the brides called I talked to them. Not text. Not sent an email. I **TALKED** to them.

I allowed them to cry, cuss, be mad, scream if they needed to and let them know that I completely understood their frustration. I didn't take anything they may have said personally because we all have been thrown into this thing without a life jacket and none of us could swim!

We were in the middle of a pandemic that the world had never seen before and with no cure, no medication, and no knowledge of what has it, or how you can catch it.

The beautiful thing about me is no matter how many times I fail I manage to get back up again stronger than ever. The House of Flawless closing isn't my first failure. Did you know that? Ohhh NO Chile… My first taste of entrepreneur life was horrible! I went out in these entrepreneur streets and got my ass handed to me! Listen! I fought a good fight, but in the end entrepreneurship kicked my ass up and down the highway… So, I knew what failure felt like… and this doesn't feel the same. This feels like a setback for a come back. This feels like a Reset, Refocus, and Restart Moment. This feels like a girl sitting down, and writing that book she was supposed to write from three years ago type moment.

This isn't a give up moment. We are in quarantine gurl! We aren't dead! WE are here, healthy (Thank God) alive, well fed (Cause I know ya'll got snacks) and kicking. Take this time of tragedy and turn it into triumph. I know you are worried and I 'm going to be transparent with you. I am too but baby we are going to make it through this. This is temporary. In the meantime, work on you.

Work on what you can while you're at home. Start on that side hustle. OWrk on revamping that website. Make those new products. Redecorate your house. Spend more time talking to your kids. Write that book. Take that class. Master your craft but for goodness sake please do not waste this precious time doing nothing.

We've never had time like this before. Don't waste it. Cherish it. Come out of this thing on another level. Come out of this thing a better you. No matter if it's with your business. Your relationship with your kids or your marriage. No matter what you need to work on... Work on it! This is the perfect time!

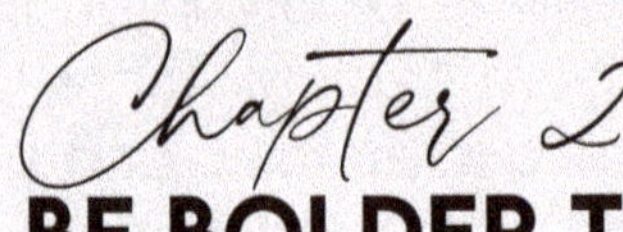

Chapter 2

BE BOLDER THEN YOUR LIPSTICK & SHARPER THAN HER EYELINER

'Just Start. Don't worry that you don't have all the answers yet.'

One day I was sitting on my couch, scrolling through my timeline on Facebook and some memories popped up from a decade ago. It was a video of me working on a photoshoot, in Lawton, Oklahoma. I sat three like "Damn" I've been doing makeup for more than 10 years now!
Where did the time go!

I reposted that video and started to write my caption. I talked about my ten year journey. Things I've been through during my freelance journey and all the lessons I've learned.

In the middle of me writing my caption it hit me! A'Lores, "Remember that book you wanted to write a few years back?" At that moment I knew I had to write my book. The time was Now!

I've put this book off for years! I wrote this idea down in my 'Goal Digger" notebook about three or four years ago, but I really didn't put forth any effort to really writing it. I would tell myself, "It's okay. You can start tomorrow."

However, when tomorrow arrived, I would find a reason to talk myself out of pursuing my goal. First thing I would say, Girl, ain't nobody going to ready a boo from you!?" What was I going to write about and then would sit there with a pen in one hand and a notebook in the other and stare at the blank pages.

Let me tell you something, self doubt is one of our most dangerous foes. So, I refused to let my own negative thoughts get the best of me. Today I decided that the only way to begin anything is to just start. So, guess what I did today, I started writing my book! I did what I did a decade ago. I took a leap and bet on myself! I 'm writing this book because I want you to do the same thing.

Start Now. Start with Fear. Start with Tears in your eyes. Start with Pain and doubt. Start with your hands shaking and your voice trembling. Start from where you are and with what you have JUST START! My thoughts stopped me for years, my self doubt stopped me for years. One thing I wanted you to do is remember you don't have to control your thoughts, but you are in charge of what thoughts you interact with and the ones that you walk away from. It's okay to say you're scared. That's a feeling and we feel that way from time to time.

This is especially true if we are doing something new but its not okay to allow those temporary feelings stop you from chasing your dreams. Believe it or not doubt and fear kills more dreams than failure ever will.

To be totally transparent with you, I wrote this book because there have been moments that I was flat out TIRED. I was tired of asking myself, "What if, What if it doesn't work, what it does work? What if people laugh? What if it flops? I got sick and tired of being an my OWN way. I got sick of me being the ONLY toxic person in the room when it came down to me achieving my dreams!

Sometimes we have to be honest with ourselves and realize the only person stopping you is the person in the mirror. When you do realize YOU are the reason why you haven't started yet when do you realize that you are self sabotaging your own success? Now, being a Beauty Expert and knowing that the lady in the mirror was doing something very unpretty things to her own life, vision and well that had to stop.

You're sitting there and you know exactly what you want to do but you're procrastinating. You're finding other things to do with your time and pretending that you're too busy to focus you're waiting until you're 100% perfect (Which will never happen by the way) until you go for it. You think you're staying nice and comfy in the comfort zone, but you aren't comfortable.

You are watching your dreams slip away. This is the mindset that some of us have and the sad thing is some of us are totally unaware that we're doing it. Take a second and think about it.

Do you display self sabotaging behavior? Before continuing to read on - just take a second to think about that. One thing I wanted us to do, and say, "Us because I'm doing it with you as I'm writing this book" but I want us to START wit self improvement. Let's start working on changing these bad and unhealthy thought patterns, negative emotions and toxic behaviors that we have.

Let's start t train our minds and our thoughts on positive thinking only. Listen! This isn't going to be easy.

Some of us have said some of the worst shit about ourselves. Some of us have had the worst thoughts about ourselves. It's time to heal from our own toxic mental state. How can you start anything with that type of thinking? Some of you will never be able to start anything for yourself because you're treating yourself worst than anyone else can treat you. You don't even feel like you can do it.

You don't feel like you're worth it. You feel like you're not good enough, pretty enough, slim enough, smart enough, wealthy enough, bold enough, or educated enough. Before ending this chapter. Want you to write an apology letter to yourself. Our STARTING point is healing ourselves. One of the most challenging things I had to learn was healing has to be intentional.

You have to come to a point that you are tired of not being bale to START because you are causing you're own misery. I 'm not going to go any further than this chapter. I want you to sharpen your pencil, be bold and I want you to write yourself an apology Letter. Don't put it off. Don't say it doesn't need to be done. Don't feel that you're going to look and sound crazy. Once again, there goes those toxic thoughts! Stop over thinking. Stop being afraid of facing the facts of how you truly think of your-self. This is the first thing I want you to do, sit back, wind down and begin. Your future start now.

"YOUR ONLY LIMIT IS YOU"

Chapter 3

"ALL YOU NEED IS LIPSTICK & LASHES"

**' If your business isn't making money,
then it isn't making sense!**

Now that we have apologized to ourselves and begun our healing process let's get to this business! What have you done to work on your business today? Did you read a book, an online story?

Did you take an online class or course? Did you make a call today about getting some guidance on how to start or did you even do any type of research on how to start?

What have you done to work on your business today?

One thing I don't want you to do is sit there and wait for someone to help you. When it come down to your business the last thing you should ever do is wait on anyone else. Do you what you need to do to get your business up and running.

"What have you done to work on your business today?"

There isn't one person out here that's going to bother helping you if you don't take the time to help yourself.

Before I really start this chapter on how you can open a successful business that's going to make you 10 million dollars in three months I should probably tell you that shit like that doesn't usually happen in real life. Unless you're a Kardashian… or Beyonce. If you are a Kardashian or Beyonce go ahead and skip the next few chapters of this book. LOL!

Starting a business is one of the most rewarding things you can do. It's also the most stressful thing you can do.

"DON'T FAKE IT TILL YOU MAKE IT. FACE IT TILL YOU MAKE IT. GET UP. WORK HARD. FAIL. STAND BACK UP AND FACE IT AGAIN.'

Don't get me wrong just because it's stressful doesn't mean you can't do it. It means that it's going to take a little more footwork and real work then you may expect. One thing I need you do do is understand is success is not overnight.

It just doesn't work that way. I don't care who you are. You have to work for it. There is no other way around it. The past decade of working in the makeup industry, I've realized that many people don't want to actually work. They want to LOOK like they're working.

If I look like I"m busy and I get a lot of likes on a picture then it makes me successful. There is a lot of faking it 'til you make it going on, but one thing I know for sure is that when the rent needs to be paid Ian't nothing fake about that. You usually can't pay your bills

with your
instagram likes and it's hard to monetize your social media comment section. When I need you to understand is that when you want to start a business it's not always going to LOOK glamorous. It's rate that you look glamorous when you are putting in hours of work. Running your own business is really some hardcore shit The hardest thing I had to get over when I opened House of Flawless was the first year. It was brand new to the city, and I wasn't from Greenville so a lot of my clients and customers came from word of mouth (which is still vital to running and sustaining a business) and then some of the customers I connected with during my makeup counter days. I had one booth renter in the building but for the rest of the bills and rent I had to make it up with product sale, and booking makeup sessions. Often, to make ends meet it was around the clock work. NO days off and barely any sleep. No kids football and basketball games. Just WORK. The crazy thing about chasing your dreams is the part of me feels like there could have been even more that I could have done to work a little harder. From the beginning I knew faking it until I made it wasn't going to work for my real life brick and mortar store. There was ALWAYS something that needed to be done.

Phone ringing, website emails, customer questions in-store, and in Facebook messenger on the business page, packing online orders, shipping them, keeping up with inventory, making sure that I was making it to all of my appointments on time, being careful not to over book, balance the bank accounts and check books, oh, and then I went home and started wit family business. This was around the clock for me and I quickly got burned out. I started to lose my love for my art of makeup. I had to find a way to balance art and business, and yes sometimes they can be one and the same but that's not how things were going for me in the first year.

It was all business. Get them in and get them out. Spend no longer than 30-45 minutes on a client because you have to more that's about to walk through the door right behind her. After my first year things started to slow down, which I was gratefully welcoming. It slowed down because I started to realize that working harder wasn't always working smarter. I was in the shop day and night, but didn't have anything to really show for it. I was still struggling to make ends meet, but I was working constantly. Then one day I had an "Ah ha moment." I was chatting with one of my friends in New York, who worked in the field of Public Relationships (D, I love you girl) I was venting. Telling her "How proud I am that the shop is doing who well, but at the same time I 'm tired, and I feel like I have nothing to show for it. I wasn't even paying myself. All the shop money went right back to the shop." She listened to me vent and whine and she immediately said, "Alores you're having this issue because you're too cheap. You're not charging your worth."

You're still charging like you're a freelance makeup artist doing makeup out of your house instead of the badass entrepreneur, certified make up artist, New York Fashion Week (2x's) work featured on Bravo Network Television Show, store owner, owning your own brand bitch that you are. Charge what you're worth.. Then add tax! I got off the phone with her and it really weighed heavy on me. I knew I was cheating myself. I knew my artistry was worth more, but what was my real issue? Why didn't I have enough confidence in myself to believe that? There was a real issue for the longest I had trouble owning who I was. I wanted people to like me. My mind was OMG! If I charge the much, people aren't going to like me.

They are not going to support my business. They are going to find the cheapest seats to sit in and I'm going to be left here in a big ass pink empty store. Now, there are some truths to that statement.

People will seek to find the cheapest seats t sit in at times, but those were not my people. Truthfully people won't like you for a number of reason and I will tell you this - what other people think about you is none of your business. Those were not the people who I aim to please.

I wanted those upscale clients, people who knew that I was worth every dime that I charged because they wanted to look FLAWLESS. The HOF client wouldn't blink an eye when I gave them everything they asked for and more. They were out there and they were willing to pay for my services because they knew that I was exceptional and most of all reliable and consistent. So, I'm saying this to you because I want you to perfect your craft so that you will be ready for them when they come. The next month my prices changed and baby, my nerves were angled and jangled.

I can remember sitting at the counter and then finally hitting that button on the website to change the price and I almost fell out of the chair. It was hilarious! I was a ball of nerves! But guess what? Clients still came, bookings started coming in within the next hour of my charging what my craft was worth. People were still calling, booking, paying deposits! It worked! Charging what I was worth **WORKED**! I think I skipped out of that shop that day, and I've been skipping ever since. I realized that I was working so hard for nickels and dimes because I was trying to make other happy and make sure they were comfortable with me, but it was at my expense. Yes, it **LOOKED** like I was booked and busy which was but the **LOOK** wasn't taking care of business. It wasn't making business sense. I needed to stop thinking like a worker and started thinking like an owner.

I heard all the time that black businesses are too expensive, but we don't have the luxury not to be. We have to twice the work, in half the time and be 20 times as good to please customers and clients, and baby don't get me wrong! Momma can do that, but you better damn sure be ready to pay for it!

That's BUSINESS sense! If you want to ever make it to those millions busting your prices down to be cheaper than your competitor is not what's going to get you there.

What it's going to get you is used, taken advantage of, played for a fool! Guess what else will happen? They will end up in the competitors chair anyway because that's what some people do. That person isn't guaranteed t one your client just because you are cheaper.

That's not what keeps client in your chair. It's your talent. It's the hard work you put into your art by mastering your craft and being ready for them when they come. It's how you make them feel when they get there and how you make them and look when they left. It's the atmosphere. It's your professionalism. It's the surroundings.

It's the education that you hav invested in your craft so you could get this far. The vibe, it's you! Don't you dare doubt your worth then you're giving your all, that is just not business sense.

Chapter 4

'WHEN LIFE GIVES YOU LEMON'S MAKE MORE LIPSTICK'

"If I live for other people's acceptance will I die from their rejection?

There was an old saying my mom use to say about people not liking me.

"Don't worry about people not liking you. Most people don't even like themselves."

I've always held on to those words because it's the God honest truth. Everybody isn't going to like you. You're not going to get a congratulations text or call. Everyone isn't going to share your story. Hell, people are even going to stop talking to you and start talking about you, but here's a question I have for you.

WHY DO THEY MATTER?

I don't remember seeing anything in the good book that God said we had to care about other people's opinions of us or that people who gossip about you will kill you, so why would you emotionally destroy yourself over other people's opinions and acceptance.

This is a question I want you to ask yourself when

dealing with the business and your personal life. One thing I've noticed over the past ten years of being in the business is that people get their panties all in a bunch if they feel like someone doesn't like them or their work. OMG! They will put on a whole show. Make shady Facebook posts towards the client. Or the next time they see the client they are nasty, halfway speak, won't speak, suck ya teeth, swing a head, roll ya eyes! Girl ya wig damn near bout to fall off cause you rolling your neck so hard! Stop! Stop it! Everybody isn't going to like your work! It's a fact. It's life. It happens! Get over it!

There are over 7 billion people in the world and you mean to tell me you 'bout ready to square up with this girl in the mall parking lot because she came to you last week and went to someone else this week because she like what the other artist did better!z She has a right to do that and how dare you take that personally.

You have other clients right!! There are other people on earth, in your state, in your city! The immediate 10 mille radius of you, but here you go. All emotionally destroyed because this one girl decided to go to someone else and not you. Now you are making shady ass Facebook post about the girl and everyone is noticing how unable you really are. Now, what you're doing is possibly running away other clients that may have thought about booking you, but they are looking at your post like NOPE! Don't have the time for the drama.

Let me ask you a question? Do you think Sephora cares about you going to Ulta after you leave their store? ≠≠No! You know why? That's because you came into Sephora, purchased what they had. PURCHASED! Spent

your
money with them! They got paid..They could care less what other store you visited after them. They could care less if you ever come back again because they know they are millions of other people walking in the door as soon as you leave. It's called minding the business that pays you! It's not your business that that girl went to someone else! You know what is your business? Making sure her debit card says "Clear" after you swipe it. Stop being so emotional. And guess what? It probably not the fact that she doesn't like your work. Maybe she just wanted to try someone new.. Maybe she wanted to support a struggling artist that was in need at the time.

Maybe she wanted a cut crease and you don't cut creases. Maybe she wanted a soft look but your work is more dramatic and hell, maybe she just didn't like her look after you were done! Whatever the reason may be its not your business!

Focus on the clients who do love you and your work. You are fighting a losing battle if you think everybody is going to love everything about you, or your work, and if you continue to think that way trust me that's going to be your downfall. Put your ego away…that bitch is toxic.

I remember doing this bridal trail for a bride that wanted me to do her wedding. We talked, and laughed during her trial. OMG we vibe like we were the best of friends. Her look was absolutely gorgeous. I had her skin laid like butter! Complexion was perfect and when I posted her pic she was the only picture I ever got over 600 likes on! When I tell ya'll I did the damn thing! I did the damn thing!

After the bridal trial I sent her my contract and prices, but never heard back from her. I would send her text messages and emails, like hey! You got the info? If you have any questions or concerns please feel free to contact me. The only thing she would say is… Okay.. Thanks. Months later while scrolling on Facebook I saw where another artist did her makeup for her wedding. My heart sank! I examined her face up, down and around… Like! EXCUSE ME! WTF! My ego started taking to me like blast that bitch! Repost her bridal trial so everybody can see you did better! Be petty and click like so she knows you see her ass! Comment under her pics. I mean my ego had me in here READY FOR WAR! LOL! I even showed her page to my husband like is she serious!!! How dare she?

Months later my email alert went off and I noticed her name in my books. I was beside myself! Oh my ego started talking again! Oh! She back huh? Why she ain't book that other artist? I need to just send her deposit back and tell her to book that other bitch! Let me find out she out here chair hopping! Honey I went on and on until the day she pulled up to the store and sat in that chair.

As soon as she sat down she said, "I'm so happy you were open to do my makeup for my baby shower! I'm so excited! I was so hurt you couldn't do my makeup for the wedding, but my husband went over the numbers for our wedding and we just had to start cutting corners. We were way over budget and I didn't want to insult you by asking for a discount or deal. I didn't want to be that bride who tried to nickel and dime you."

To find out her cousin was in school to be an aesthetician and she VOLUNTEERED to do her makeup for her. Let me tell ya'll something…I felt like SHIT! Do you HEAR ME!! SHIT! I sat here and called that girl everything but the child of God!

I think I even deleted the girl info out my phone! I think I blocked her! I ain't even offer the girl a bottle of water when she walked in and saw she was hot and pregnant!! Ya'll, my heart stopped beating! My eyes got all watery. I couldn't even look that girl in the eye. I was ASHAMED because I allowed my ego and my emotions to tell me what I'm so entitled to someone and their business and when I don't get that person I caught a full fledge temper tantrum and conducted myself in the most unprofessional way possible. Who the F do I think I am? Baby Jesus in the manager? At that moment I took my emotion, and ego out of my business. I went back and asked myself why did I get so upset? Why did I feel so rejected when I saw that she choose another artist for her wedding day.

Have you ever noticed how you feel when you post a picture on your social media and start to get tons of likes, hearts and comments? How does it make you feel? Good, right? Like ayeeeee! And God forbid if you go viral! Babaeeee! at this point you are a guru and nobody can tell you nothing! That feeling of acceptance and being liked takes over us. They like me!z Look at all this attention I'm getting, and then you start getting this ego!z You went from they like me to who got check me boo?!

Then you forget what the world humble means. Shit at this point you don't even remember how to spell it. Then one day the likes stop. The shares stop. You can't even buy a like... The attention is gone and you start acting out and acting crazy just to get some type of attention. Do you know why you're doing that? Because you have attached yourself to this unreal social media society that will drop you at any second. You've invested your entire being into this world of being accepted by people you don't even know and now you are lost, depressed and feeling like your worth is gone.

So, do me a favor, give this some thought - "If I live for
their acceptance, will I die from their rejection?"

You must accept yourself before the instagram likes and
Facebook comments you must accept and love yourself
first. Love your art, your body, your hair, and your look.
Love the way you talk and walk. You must love and accept
you so when rejection comes knocking at your door you
can continue to stand up tall without falling apart. Without
worrying about what others are saying. Without your ego
causing a scene. Without depression. You can stand there
and say I could care less who does or doesn't accept me
cause Babeeeaa! I 'm the shit **REGARDLESS**!!

Chapter 5

When I first started doing makeup it was not the popular thing to do. I would post my looks on Facebook and it would drive people crazy. OMG, A'Lores what are you doing? Why are you wearing makeup? Holy Shit, she's doing too much. They would laugh. Ohhhh, and affording to my Facebook messages, some women were even concerned that I was having a nervous breakdown. What was truly sad was that it was actually so funny to them. My pictures would get passed around just so they could make fun of me. Mind you I didn't start off as a level 10 artist (rarely does anyone start at the top of their game) but even if

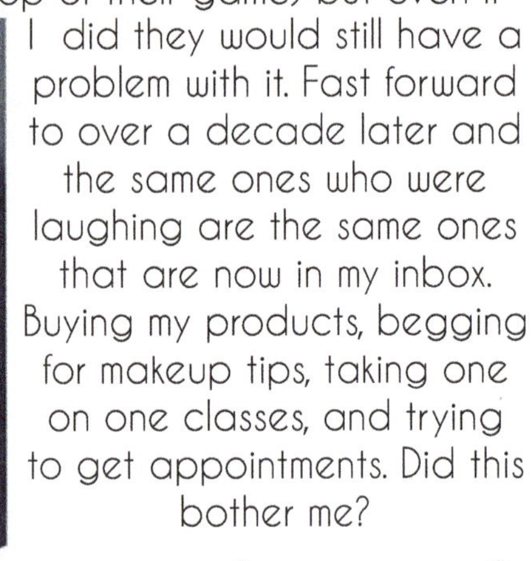

I did they would still have a problem with it. Fast forward to over a decade later and the same ones who were laughing are the same ones that are now in my inbox. Buying my products, begging for makeup tips, taking one on one classes, and trying to get appointments. Did this bother me?

Yes! Ten years ago if you would have told me the ones that were laughing are now some of the same ones beating down my doors I would have thought you were crazy.

Unfortunately, sometimes this is what people do. Sometimes things that are unfamiliar to people they tend to diminish, pick at or even laugh at. Sometimes, you will find yourself being treated like you have absolutely no business doing what makes you feel good! It's kind of like how DARE she?! How dare she sit over there and not be like everyone else?! Who told her she could get those up and down nasty looks - do you because trust me, they are laughing now but they will be copying later.

That's the mindset of certain people, they have to wait for something to get popular before others validate the exceptional product that you create, and then they tend to follow, and that's okay! Let them follow your lead. Let them copy because you're the leader. You are the trendsetter. DO you seriously think everything trendsetter that's hit it big didn't start off being laughed out of the building? That they weren't told, "NO" This is your journey and you are built to handle it.

Fun Facts: Did you know Walt Disney was fired from the Kansas City Star because they editor said, and I quote "Walk Disney lacked Imagination!" Marilyn Monroe was so before her time when she first started modeling and acting the agencies told her she should look into being a secretary. In high school, Michael Jordan was cut from the basketball team. I said THEEE MICHAEL JORDAN! Jennifer Hudson was voted off American Idol and if I 'm not mistaken Simon Cowell didn't care too much for her voice and had to apologize when she won her Oscar. Jay-Z (One of the best Lyricist in my opinion) could not get one single person to buy his first Cd… He had to sell it out of his car. Now, this man is worth $1 Billion! We also should never forget that Oprah was fired from her first job on television because she was too unconventional as a reporter. Look how that turned out.

This is how it all begins. This is the journey. SO allow me to motivate you. Let these stories fuel your creativity and encourage you to keep doing YOU. I will never forget the day I handed in my 2 week notice at Belk and my counter Manager said, "So, What are you going to do n ow?" I said I was going to own up my own cosmetics store. She looked me dead in my eyes, laughed and said, "Oh, you'll be back!" Guess where she is now?

Working at some clothing store downtown, following my instagram, watching me Wednesday mornings on Channel 7 news giving the Week It Wednesday makeup tips, while running my cosmetic store, and my exclusive House of Flawless Brand which just celebrated its 3 year anniversary… get my drift? So, when they laugh at you, your weirdness and big dreams make sure to laugh with them because they have absolutely no idea that ten years from now they are going to be asking you for your autograph, assistance, or even your products.

First they laugh then they Copy

How many times do you say that word in a day? Do you say it to your kids, your family members, co-workers? Are you comfortable with the word, "No?" Does the word NO upset you, scare you, or intimidate you? Not me! No is one of my favorite words. A'lores can I borrow a few dollars? No! A'lores can I get a discount? No! A'Lores can we collaborate? NO, NO and may I add NOO! I 'm not saying that to be mean. I 'm really not. I 'm saying no because when you say yes to everything you will truly get yourself into a bind that you can't get out of. I learned to say NO without feeling guilty. I used to think that saying no would mean that I'm rude, but you know that you can say no and still have a good heart? Saying no shows that you respect healthy boundaries.

I LEARNED TO SAY NO WITHOUT FEELING GUILTY

Being a woman and running a business we get this BITCH stamp on our forehead for using the word NO and a lot of woman are afraid to have that stamp. There are so many women out there that are running crazy and stressed out because they are saying yes to everything, trying to be liked by everyone and stretching themselves thin. You don't even have time for yourself because you are Yes'ing every damn body. You are doing this in your personal life and you're doing this in your business life and you're driving yourself insane. Say this with me.... Saying the work No does not make me a bad person.

Saying the word No does not mean you don't care. The word NO is a form of self care. Please don't have this idea in your head that if you continue to say yes to people you are going to be on everyone's good side. What you're doing is setting yourself up to be used and your kindness being taken advantage of.

Being the one that everyone uses does not make you well liked, or more successful. It makes you a TARGET. While growing your business you must know who to say NO to and who to say Yes to. While I've learned the art of saying no, I've also learned the art of saying Yes. I've always asked myself a group of questions before giving my answer. Will doing this make me feel good or happy about it? Do I have time to commit myself to something like that? How will this project or collaboration benefit me as well as the other person?

I've learned to really sit down and ask myself these questions before saying yes t anything that's presented to me. You will notice how your business flourishes so much more when you don't say YES to everything that's being thrown your way.

For example, there was a young artist that just started doing makeup and she reached out to me asking me a few questions about a project she committee to. She was so excited because she was chosen to be a makeup artist in a fashion show. I was happy for her but I can tell she was a little unsure about it. She started talking about how many people she had to do and how low the pay was...

Nobody was going to drive to me to get their makeup done after the show was over. Not because I wasn't good enough, but my location wasn't convenient enough to win over Dallas clients. So, I came home with used products in my kits, an empty gas tank, tired as hell, no clients and shit I don't even remember getting a thank you after the show was over. I got a BYE! We're gonna call you next year! Did they call? Yes... did I return the call, NO! This happens to most of us who are trying to start our career. Some people call it paying our dues, but when is the damn dues paid?? When do you realize you are playing yourself for likes and hoping that it will work out. Listen, don't think I'm sitting here saying don't do any fashion shows. I've done all the fashion shows!

I worked New York Fashion week twice. However, you should participate in these events not because you want to gain more experience and not because you're expecting some kind of come up. DO it for all the beautiful memories you will make and the amazing friendships that will be created.

Now, there was a time when I said yes, and it worked out very well for me. This was when I sued to mix my lipsticks all the time and a very popular artist wanted to use my lipsticks in class... I'll never forget. I mixed 150 hippies for this class. She used them in her class and passed them out to everyone who attended. I got followers, some clients and my website started to blow up with shoppers and sales. Some of those shoppers and followers still shop with me to this day and that was 5-6 years ago. That's what got my lipstick line off the ground. Fast Forward to a few months ago a very popular blogger requested that I send her 100 of my lipsticks for her event... ummm HELL NO! LMBO!! Do you know how much money I'm sending off! I'm not mixing things anymore... now we're talking manu-facturing, labeling, shipping and packaging!!!z GIRL BYE!!! On top of that I sent this same blogger every color in my entire line, a few months before she sent this request, she wore one, posted it in her stories and I got not ONE sale from that.

Why would I turn around and send her 100 more lipstick. That's not business savvy and if I was too scared to tell her No I would have stressed myself trying to send her $1890.00 worth of products and worrying myself to sleep about how I'm going to bounce back from that if I got no sales from her event. Yes, I may have gotten a couple of followers but as a business owner you have to understand that followers don't always equal money... I'm not digging into that right now. That's the next chapter.. but baby followers don't always equal money, and I know a lot of you are thinking. A'lores, but you said she was a popular blogger. What if you sent her your lipsticks and your sales would have gone through the roof.

Well, let's think back. I sent her my entire collection a few months before her request. She posted one of them. ONE and blogged about one color to the followers and that was that. NO sales came from that. A few followers, but no customers. So if she couldn't sell one Lipstick to a million of her followers why would I load 100 of her followers up with $1890 full of products in a free goodie bag in hopes that they come back and purchase. The only one that's benefiting is her with me footing the bill.

Just like they say you have to pick and choose your battles. That goes the same way with your Yes,'s. Hand those yes's out like they're gold from God's pearly gates! Treat them like they are precious to your soul.

This was the beginning of me opening my store and I didn't mind the only person who would have gotten anything from this would have been her. So, I respectfully and graciously declined. I explained I'm opening my store (which she already knew because we talked about it.) and I just couldn't jump in any deal that didn't help me with my business. My time, and my resources were all tied up into the House of Flawless right now. Do you know I never heard from that woman again? My mentor. The one I admired so much. The one who could and did call me anytime she needed and I was there. I gave her one NO and she cut me off completely.

When I had my grand opening for the store she never even so much sent a congratulations text. I was heartbroken. Who knew the world NO would hurt so much. I thought so highly of her and I didn't want to lose her as a mentor and a friend not realizing she was never really down for me to begin with. Even though my loyalty and love ran deep for her she could have cared less. It wasn't about what I was doing for her. It was about what she could get out of me and once that well ran dry she was done. I blamed myself for her behavior. I didn't set boundaries between our business or our friendship.

I made her feel so entitled and so privilege in my life that when I was finally wanted to do something for myself she was insulted that I actually wanted to start improving my life, living my dream, reaching my goals, instead of running behind her hand and foot.

Even though this hurt me to my core it was a lesson that needed to be learned. You can't let other people set the agenda for your life. It's okay to say no to your friends, and someone you love. It's okay to say no to mentors and people you look up to. It's okay to say no to a parent or your kids. Even if it may hurt someone's feelings or make the conversation uncomfortable.

You're allowed to set limitations and boundaries.

Don't compromise yourself to make someone else happy. It's okay to take care of yourself and if that means saying "No" you have every right to do so. Saying no is the highest form of self love and respect.

Chapter 7

IT'S NOT YOU! IT'S YOUR LIPSTICK!

Her wins do not mean you lose so clap for her! You two aren't even in the same race.

Do you have that competitive streak in you, Sis? If so, lose it. You around here competing and looking crazy in the process. You competing with you, ya neighbor, ya business partner, ya friends, ya co-workers, the pastor, ya boyfriend, his momma, ya half great great auntie on your grandma side twice removed, ya Facebook friends, ya instagram

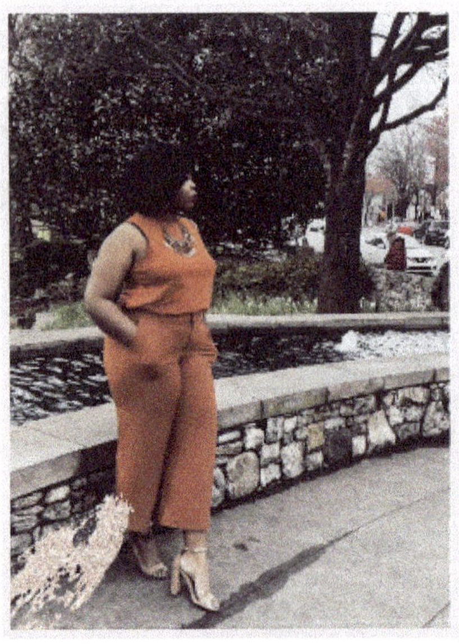

enemies, hell you even trying to compete against Jesus and **HE WALKED ON WATER**! He raised the dead, made a blind man see and you're out here competing trying to make sure the people see you put your foot in that water!!! You look foolish and just because you're being clapped on and laugh WITH that doesn't mean you're necessarily being supported. Your being extra loud to be seen but are you being booked. I love to sit back and watch people, Yes, I'm a people watcher. I watch reactions and things people will do for attention, but what I am not is a competitor.

What I will **NOT** do is compete with one living soul on this earth! I'm am in competition with no one. I have absolutely no desire to play the game of being better than anyone. I'am simply trying to be better than me.

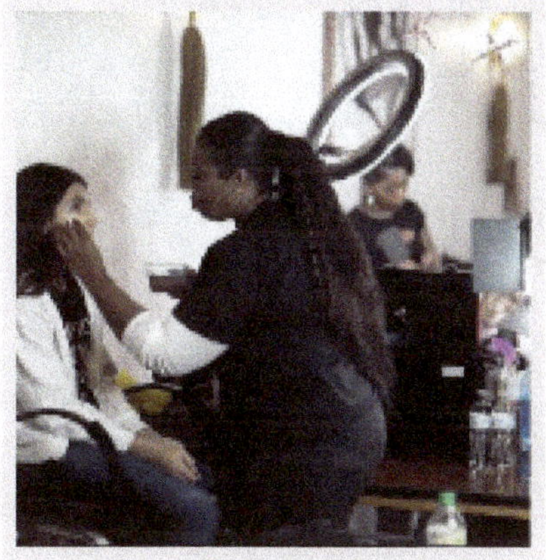

The sad thing is many people that live to
compete against others
need to realize that other
people aren't your
competition. Your
competition is your
procrastination.

Your ego.
The amount of unhealthy
food you're feeding your
thoughts, the knowledge you
neglect, the negative
behavior you're nurturing
and your lack of creativity.
Instead of
continuously thinking
of ways to be compete
against others may find a
way to COLLAB. Coming
together as a team.

Try to remember that your
only competition should be
the person looking back at
you when you're in the mirror.
Not the person
beside you or the one
who is genuinely trying to
help you. Your confidence
shouldn't come from thinking oh! I'm better than her,
but your confidence should
come from yes! I'm great

and so is she! I 'm not going to focus on this chapter too long or harp on the subject but I do want to leave this one last thought in your mind. We should be lifting each other up, cheering each other on. Not trying to outshine one another. The sky would be awfully dark with just one star.

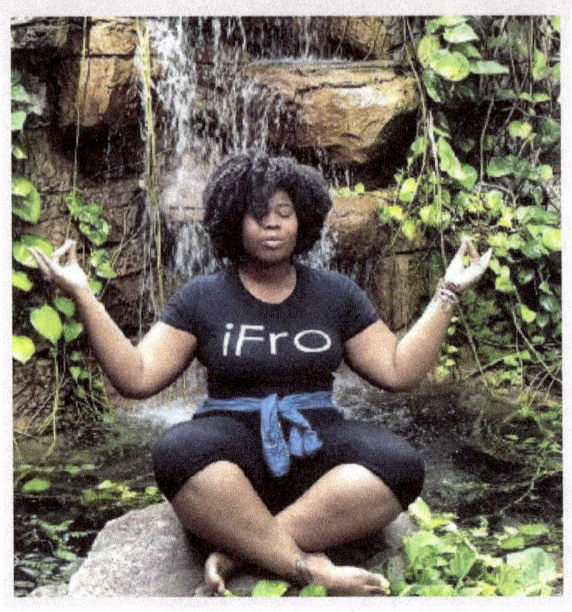

Chapter 8
COLORFUL MANIFESTATIONS
& MAGENTA MEDITATIONS.

Several years ago I toyed with the idea of having my own store. I wasn't even calling it a store. I was calling it a studio. I would tell a friend here or there yes I want my own studio one day, but never really looked into getting one. I built my clientele one person at a time. Took on counter job after counter job but never really thought I was ready for my own. Not until I had that failing moment. I talked about that on the About Me page. That night I sat down and wrote in my journal what I wanted to do. I wrote down everything that could come to my mind. From making a million dollars with my cosmetic line to opening my store, to writing a book… as of right now 2 of those things have come into fruition. You're reading the book now and the store has been open for three years.

"Write it down on a real piece of paper, with a real pen

and watch shit get real" - Erykah Badu

I created what I wanted out of my life by writing it down, but I did not just simply write it down and walked away, but I thought about it. I thought about what I wanted to create and manifest. I visualized myself already in my store, I visualized myself already being one of the best selling authors on Amazon, New York Best Sellers, USA Today Best Selling book List and on Oprah's Book Club as a MUST READ, oh and let's not forget Target Book Shelves.

I'm literally manifesting that as I'm writing this book today. I can see it. I can touch it so it will be mine. There's no doubt in my mind, no negative thoughts in my head, and no fear in my heart only faith. Only the feeling I have is of accomplishment and me Thanking God for what's already been done. Mountains have already been moved for me. The book is already on the shelves of Barnes & Nobles. You will see it as soon as you walk in the door. Can you see it? I can. I already manifested it. It's already there. I've already created it, written it down and now it's time for me to watch and RECEIVE all that's coming my way.

During this chapter the only thing I want you to do is create the reality you want to live. I don't care if it's something big or something small. I don't care if it's a free cup of coffee or an entire coffee shop. I want you to create your reality. Some people find this hard because this takes quieting your mind, putting your phone down and unplugging your thoughts from your surroundings. Let's say you have a bill that's due. I don't need you to focus on the bill the's due. I need to focus on the fact the same bill has already been paid. I want you to thank god for the bill being paid. I want you to visualize the Thank you for your payment email. You can't do this by thinking but A'Lores, I don't have the money. I didn't ask you that. I didn't ask you to visualize how you were going to get the money.

I asked you to visualize the bill already being paid. Let me tell you a little story about how The House of Flawless manifested. This is a true story. I was working in a salon downtown Greenville and it went from Sugar to shit real quick! I packed all my things and left! I went home feeling defeated.I failed at my first taste of being my own boss and now I 'm out here with a ton of clientele but no home for them. So, what did I do?

I regrouped. I made the extra bedroom I had in my house my makeup room and went to work. Not only was I taking clients there but I was meditating and manifesting at the same time.

Every morning I would wake up. Fix myself a cup of coffee, sit in the middle of my makeup room and visualize myself in the middle of my makeup store. One thousand square feet, pink walls, white and goal dressing, pretty little qhit pillow all over, cute wall pictures that said 'Hello Beautiful', 'House of Flawless lipstick in all colors, and an area for myself and other makeup artists that needed a home. I mediated on this every morning for nine months straight. I thanked God for blessing me with my own store and I thanked God for the money that would be made, the bills that were already paid and the faces that were going to be laid honey!

The store was already mine. Along with the mediation came work because we all know that faith without works is dead. So, I continued to work on my clients from home but I also found a real estate agent that would help me look for my store. We would walk downtown Greenville and Simpson-ville and look at empty stores each week. We would go to different locations and go over the pricing until one day I finally found the spot. One thousand square feet. Down-town Simpsonville as soon as I walked in the door I knew it was mine. Not because of the location, or even the de-cor inside because the decor was NOT like it is now! LOL!

But I knew it was mine because when you looked into the back of the store where the back door was there was stain glass window. I call them church window and the stained glass had a white dove in the middle of the design. There was something about this window that spoke to me. I took a picture and sent it to my mom. She texted back immediately saying, 'THAT'S YOUR STORE!" Guess what though. I DIDN'T HAVE ANY MONEY!

Yes, I was still taking clients at home, but that didn't even cover the first month rent and security deposit that's not even counting inventory, but without hesitation I told the owner of the shop to give me three weeks. That night I went back in prayer and deep meditation. Not only did I need money, I needed inventory, I needed enough clients and customers to keep the doors open, I needed artist that wanted to work there, I needed support from a city who really didn't know me. I needed HELP but when I prayed and mediated I didn't focus on what I needed. I thank God for what I had.

See, God already gave me the store. The white dove in the window was my sign of my new beginning, peace, love and prosperity. So, I knew the store was mine. I also knew that God would not give me a whole store without all the bells and hustles to go with it. So, when I prayed and meditated I thanked God for the support of the city, I thanked god for all the help he sent my way during the opening, I thanked God for the clients, and customers. I thanked him for the opening those doors and most of all I thank God for sending me the money needed for inventory, first month rent and security deposit.

Every morning during my meditation the store was already open and booming. Within two weeks the money for rent and the security deposit hit my account. Four days later

28K hit my account. TWENTY-EIGHT THOUSAND DOLLARS. That money was for inventory, decorating the store, and 7k for savings. One week later the landlord decided he would paint the store for me and redo the floors for me (which was not in the contract) free of charge. A few weeks later The House of Flawless was opened for business. The grand opening was magical. The store was packed, foundations were flying off the shelves, and I sold out of lipstick that same night. This caught the eye of Fox Carolina News who came to the shop to do a story on The House of Flawless.

This caught the eye of Sheen Magazine who also came into the store to do a interview. This caught the Eye of Scene on 7 in Greenville, SC who wanted me to do a studio interview which has led me to a steady gig on their Work It Wednesday news segments that i'v been doing the past three years.

Those opportunities led to the BET awards, NBA awards and being endorse by brand names such as Clinique, whom partnered with the House of Flawless for our first beauty event, Amazing Cosmetics, Juvia's Place, Inglot, Embryolisse, and many other big brands. My reach goes far as Becca, Bare Minerals, Dermalogica, and many more. Prayer got me here. Meditation brought it to me. Doing the work allowed me to make it happen and I watched it all manifest right before my eyes. Tonight before bed write down everything you want in your new reality. Don't worry about how you're going to get it. Just write it down. While you're writing, make sure to visualize it. I don't care how crazy you think it is. Write it down. IF yo want a 10 million dollar house. Write it down. If you want to meet Beyonce. Write it down. IF you want your own business, shop, book, new car, becoming a makeup mogul, model, top hair stylist, top earning YouTuber on Youtube, baddest makeup artist that walks on the face of the earth.

WRITE. IT. DOWN!

Visualize yourself already there, work on becoming what you want to become and sit back and watch it happen. Don't let anyone tell you it's crazy. Don't let anyone tell you it's an unrealistic goal. Your meditations and manifestations aren't for anyone else but you. Your New life & Dreams are out there waiting for you. It's just waiting for you to manifest it.

Chapter 9
NEVER UNDERESTIMATE THE POWER OF PINK LIPSTICK AND HIGH HEELS.
Repeat after me, Yes, the FUCK you can!

Excuse me Gurl! Have you forgotten who you are? Have you forgotten how flaw-some you are?(flawless: an individual who embraces their flaws and knows they are awesome anyway) You are a glow-getter! A busy woman who knows her worth. Slays her goals, and leaves a glow on the other women everywhere he goes. You carry courage above fear. You are sunshine mixed with a little hurricane. Baby Girl! You are a FUCKING BEAST! You are learning to stand strong in what you feel and what you want. You are powerful, unstoppable, a beautiful, talented woman. You get on your shit, stay on your shit, stay out of shit and don't tell people shit so explain something to me? Why are you doubting yourself? You do know your current situation is not your final destination right? So, I ask you again have you forgotten who you are?

Your ancestors did not manifest themselves into your soul to watch you become a convenient place for someone else's feet.
My dear you are a queen.

You are stronger than you think you are. I just need you to get out of your own way and remember that. Tonight for this chapter let's journal. Let's take the time to talk to ourselves and remember who we are. Let's take a moment to remember that we can do anything we set our mind to.

I need you to know that regardless of where you've been planted you are going to blossom because you are the type of flower that still grows after a forest fire.

You are stronger than you think you are!

Chapter 10

WHEN LIFE GIVES YOU LEMONS, APPLY MORE LIPSTICK
The final break down...

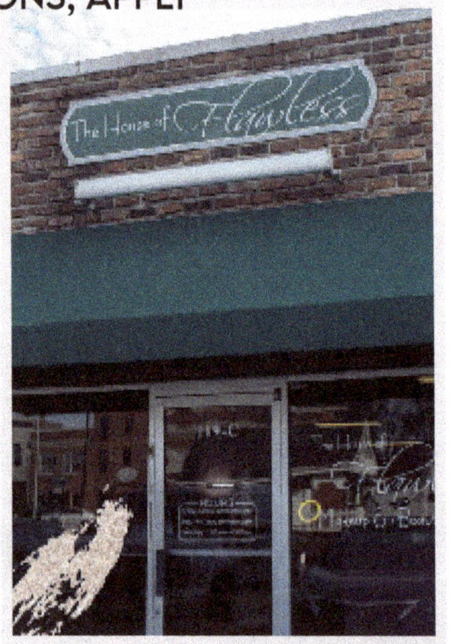

At this moment for this chapter I decided to write in the middle of my store. As soon as I walked in Could smell the sweet smell of good vibes, and success that once lived here before COVID-19. The only thing I could do was melt down and cry. God! What's next?? What was God trying to tell me??

I often asked this question especially with the passing of my mother back in August. My mom was taken, my business brought to a sudden halt, and my mind often playing tricks on me. I became paranoid that friends, family and associates were on some shady shit, exhausted from stressing and worrying. My patience became non-existent and my faith shaken. God, what are you trying to tell me? What's next? As the tears filled in my eyes I hear a sweet voice that says, "You are here and I'm giving your time. What's next is whatever you want it to be! If you want to shut down. Then shut down. IF you want to switch it up, then switch it up. If you want to expand. EXPAND! This is your journey. I have given you the gift of time so you can sit still and see what's right there in front of you.

I've given you gift of time so you can stop ignoring the signs of unreliable friends, toxic relationships, the mismanagement of funds. I've given you this time so you can see exactly how much your husband truly loves you. It's time for you to sit back and watch how hard he works just to make sure you have what you want and need. You always knew this but it's time for you to open your eyes and actually see what he goes though for the love his family.

Your marriage, your love, and union needed this time. I've gifted you this time so you can tap back into those gifts I blessed you with and enjoy the moments you have with your children. They so desperately needed your time because at one point business always took the front seat in your life and they always got the leftovers.

I have gifted you with this time so you can properly grieve because all your mother wanted was time, but you rarely had time for her when she was here and now it's your time to deal with ti. I'm giving you time to talk to me. When was the last time we walked? When was the last time we spoke quietly without being rushed? When was the last time you've been able to actually listen to me without my words being distorted. your spiritually and your soul need-

ed this time. This isn't a punishment. This is a blessing that you will never see again.

This isn't time for you to break down but to stand up. This is time for you to remember who you are and what I 'v given you. You're not

hopeless, and if you want life, liberty and the pursuit of happiness then this is your time to
GET UPand GET IT.

CPSIA information can be obtained
at www.ICGtesting.com
Printed in the USA
BVHW061000210321
603097BV00009B/1770